PET

William Shakespeare

Nina Morgan

WAYLAND

Titles in the Life and Times series:

Florence Nightingale • Queen Elizabeth I • Queen Victoria • William Shakespeare •

First published in 1998 by Wayland Publishers Limited, 61 Western Road, Hove, East Sussex BN3 1JD

Copyright © Wayland Publishers Limited 1998

British Cataloguing in Publication Data
Morgan, Nina
William Shakespeare. - (Life and Times)
1. Shakespeare, William - 1564 - 1616 – Biography – Juvenile literature
2. Great Britain – History – Elizabeth – 1588 - 1603 – Juvenile literature
3. Great Britain – James I – Juvenile literature
I. Title
822.3 ' 3

ISBN 0 7502 2293 X

Typeset in England by Joyce Chester
Printed and bound in Italy
by G. Canale & C.S.p.A, Turin

Editor: Carron Brown/Elizabeth Gogerly
Consultant: Norah Granger
Cover designer: Jan Sterling
Text designer: Joyce Chester
Production controller: Carol Stevens

Picture acknowledgements

The publishers would like to thank the following organizations for allowing their pictures to be reproduced in this book: Bridgeman Art Library/Private collection title page, 22, /Victoria & Albert Museum, London 5, /British Library, London 6, 10, 25 /Dulwich Picture Gallery, London 19; E.T. Archive 17, 20; Mary Evans Picture Library 11, 15, 16, 24, 27; Getty Images 4, 8, 13; Ronald Grant Archive 28; Robert Harding /Peter Scholey 7; The Kobal Collection/Columbia 21; National Portrait Gallery 18; Photostage/Donald Cooper 26; Topham Picturepoint 9, 23, 29 (both); Wayland Picture Library cover, 4, /Richard Hook 14 (bottom), 26.

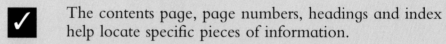

Find Wayland on the Internet at http://www.wayland.co.uk

All Wayland books encourage children to read and help them improve their literacy.

✓ The contents page, page numbers, headings and index help locate specific pieces of information.

✓ The glossary reinforces alphabetic knowledge and extends vocabulary.

✓ The further information section suggests other books dealing with the same subject.

✓ Find out more about how this book is specifically relevant to the National Literacy Strategy on page 31.

Contents

Life in Elizabethan times

When Elizabeth I was Queen, England became one of the most powerful countries in the world. People were proud to be English.

Elizabethan sailors and traders crossed oceans and explored new lands. Musicians and writers wrote new songs and plays for the Queen to enjoy.

▲ Elizabeth I liked to dress well and her clothes were often decorated with jewels.

▲ Elizabeth I enjoyed watching Shakespeare's plays.

Elizabeth I became Queen of England in 1533, and ruled until she died in 1603.

But for ordinary people, life in Elizabethan times was hard. Most people lived in the countryside. When crops failed, they starved or walked to towns to try and beg for a living.

▲ Country people worked very hard to survive.

Young William

William Shakespeare was born in 1564 in Stratford-upon-Avon in Warwickshire. No one knows his exact birthday but he was baptized on 26 April, at Holy Trinity Church in the town.

William's birthplace in Stratford. ▼

William was the third child of John and Mary Shakespeare. John was a leatherworker. He was also an alderman and an important man in the town. This meant that William could study at the local grammar school.

Elizabethan aldermen. ▶

An early marriage

When William was 18 years old, he married Anne Hathaway, the daughter of a local landowner.

The couple lived with William's parents and William worked with his father. Their daughter Susanna was born in May, 1583.

A family group painted in Shakespeare's time. The children were dressed like grown-ups. ▼

▲ Anne's house before she married William.

A few years later William decided to go to London. Nobody knows why William left Stratford. Anne stayed in the town all her life.

Shakespeare lived in London without his family for nearly 20 years.

London plays

In London Shakespeare joined a group of actors called the Chamberlain's Men. They rented a playhouse called the Theatre. Shakespeare worked as an actor and wrote plays.

Groups of actors travelled all over the country. ▼

▲ Actors performed
at theatres, inns or
private houses.

No one knows when Shakespeare started
writing plays or what his first play was
called. He usually wrote one or two
plays each year. By the end of his life, he
had written thirty-seven plays in all.

In Shakespeare's
time there were
several theatres
in London, but
most actors
performed their
plays in the
yards of inns.

Visiting the family

While he lived in London Shakespeare could only visit his family during Lent. At this time all types of public entertainments were banned and all the theatres were closed.

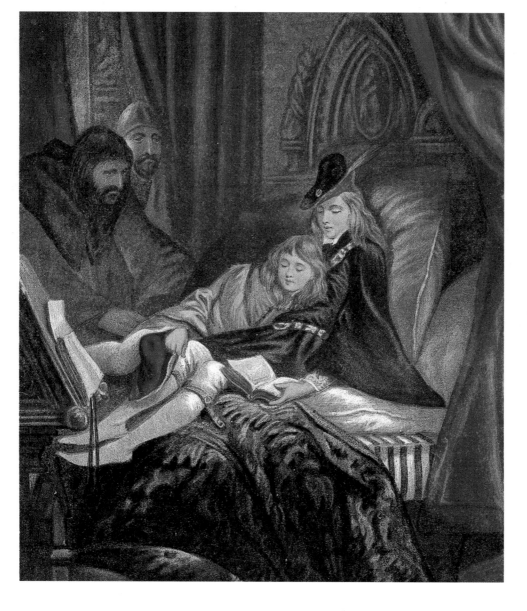

◀ Shakespeare's play, *Richard III*, told the story of the murder of these young princes.

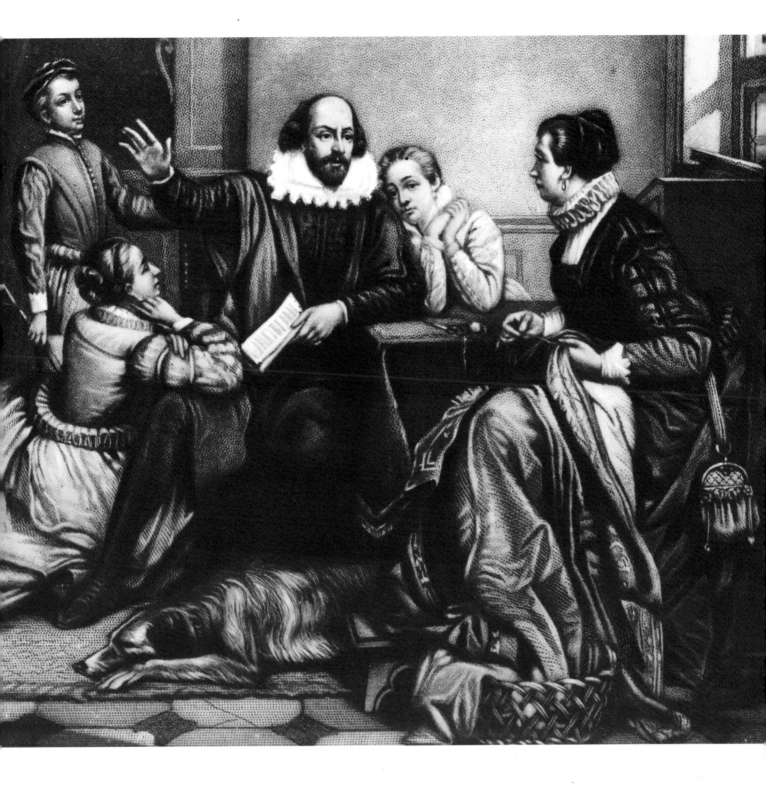

In 1585, William and Anne had twins. They called the boy Hamnet and the girl Judith. But Hamnet died when he was just eleven years old.

▲ Shakespeare enjoyed reading his plays to the family.

The plague

In 1592 the plague broke out in London. This awful disease killed thousands of people. To stop the disease spreading all the theatres in London were closed down.

▲ Large graves were made for people who died of the plague.

▲ Shakespeare wrote 154 beautiful poems called Sonnets.

◀ The Earl of Southampton helped and encouraged Shakespeare.

The theatres were closed for more than a year. During this time Shakespeare wrote poems. Some of his most popular poems were called Sonnets. He often wrote these for his friends. When the theatres reopened Shakespeare wrote plays again.

Shakespeare's first poems were about Greek myths. They were written for the Earl of Southampton.

A theatre of their own

In 1598 the Theatre was shut down. The Chamberlain's Men couldn't find another theatre so they decided to build their own new playhouse. They named it the Globe.

▼ The Globe Theatre in Shakespeare's day.

The Globe had room for more than 3,000 people. The first play performed there was Shakespeare's Julius Caesar.

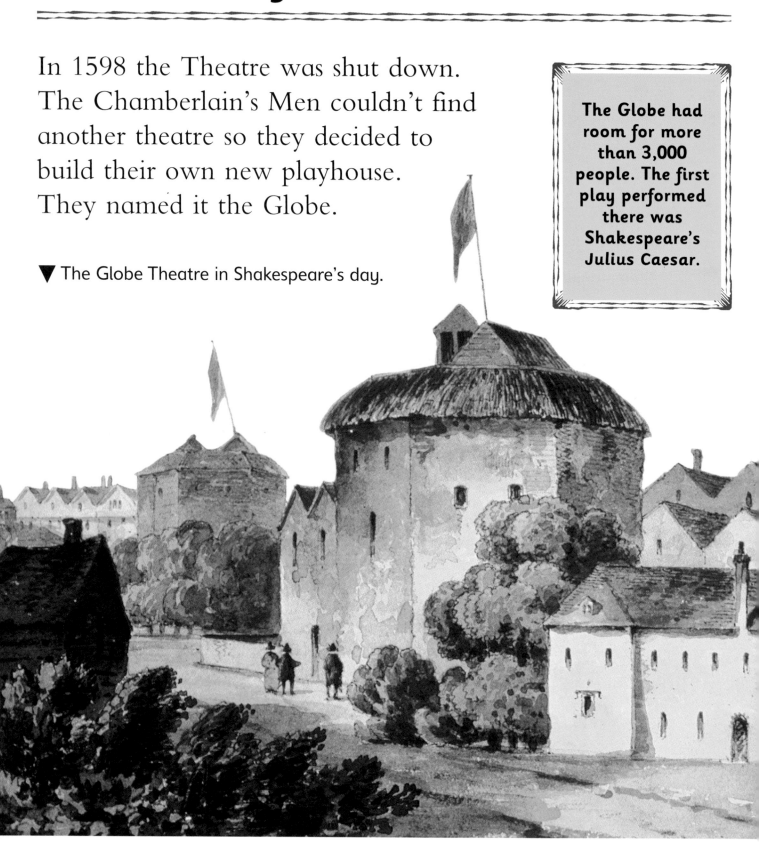

Shakespeare wrote many of the plays performed at the Globe. This is a scene from *Henry IV*. ▶

The Globe was built on the south bank of the River Thames. It was one of London's finest theatres.

The actors used their own money to build the theatre. But later they shared the money they collected from the performances of the plays.

The King's men

When James I became King of England in 1603, the Chamberlain's Men changed their name to the King's Men.

◀ When Elizabeth I died James VI of Scotland became James I of England.

They soon became the King's favourites. He paid them well for their performances. He gave them each lengths of red cloth so that they could wear his royal livery.

They wore this uniform in public to show that they were the King's servants.

The members of the King's Men changed over the years. Here are some of their names:

Richard Burbage,
John Heminge,
Henry Condell,
John Lowin,
Augustine Phillips,
George Bryan,
Will Kemp,
Laurence Fletcher
and William Shakespeare.

▲ The actor Richard Burbage helped to build the Globe Theatre.

Life in Stuart times

When James became King, life began to change in England. He liked ideas and fashions from other countries. He became known for spending money on himself and his favourites, rather than on his people. James was not well liked by the English people but he reigned for many years.

◄ James I asked the King's Men to provide the entertainment at his daughter's wedding.

◀ Shakespeare's *Macbeth* was about a Scottish king.

Shakespeare wrote new types of plays to please the King. These plays were often serious and told about troubled times.

Back to Stratford

In 1613, the Globe was burnt to the ground during a performance of *Henry VIII*. No one died in the fire. It was a sad time for Shakespeare and the King's Men.

By 1613 Shakespeare was visiting Stratford more often. At last, he could spend more time with his family. He was 49 years old, and a rich and important man of the town. He owned houses and land.

▲ Shakespeare and other famous writers from his time.

Shakespeare died at home in Stratford-upon-Avon in 1616. He was buried in Holy Trinity Church. When he died, the King's Men were the most famous company of actors in the country.

▲ Holy Trinity Church now. It has hardly changed since Shakespeare's day.

The plays in print

After William Shakespeare died the King's Men published all his plays together in one book. This was not an easy job because all of Shakespeare's own copies of the plays were lost. It was fortunate that the actors could still remember most of the words.

▲ The plays were printed at a printing house like this one.

MR. WILLIAM
SHAKESPEARES
COMEDIES,
HISTORIES, &
TRAGEDIES.

Published according to the True Originall Copies.

LONDON
Printed by Isaac Iaggard, and Ed. Blount. 1623.

The plays were finally published in 1623 in a book called *Mr William Shakespeare's Comedies, Histories, & Tragedies*. This book is known as the First Folio.

▲ The title page of the First Folio.

Comedy, tragedy or history?

In the First Folio, John Heminge and Henry Condell grouped Shakespeare's plays into three sections called comedies, tragedies and histories.

▲ A modern actor plays the part of the King in Richard II.

◀ King Richard II was the subject of one of Shakespeare's history plays.

▲ A performance of *A Midsummer Night's Dream*, one of Shakespeare's comedies.

The histories, such as *Richard II*, tell exciting stories about real events in the past. The tragedies, such as *Hamlet*, usually have very sad endings. The comedies, such as *A Midsummer Night's Dream*, tell funny stories.

The plays live on

Shakespeare's plays are still very popular. His works are enjoyed all over the world. They have been translated into different languages and performed in theatres, or on television and radio. Many of them have been made into exciting films.

The tragedy *Romeo and Juliet* was recently made into a film. ▼

▲ Inside the new Globe Theatre in London.

In 1997 a new Globe theatre was opened in London. There people can enjoy Shakespeare's plays, just as they did in this famous playwright's own day.

▲ Shakespeare's characters live on!

Timeline

1558 Elizabeth I becomes Queen of England.

1564 (April) William Shakespeare is born in Stratford-upon-Avon.

1582 William Shakespeare marries Anne Hathaway.

1583 Their daughter, Susanna, is born.

1585 Their twins, Judith and Hamnet, are born.

1596 Hamnet dies.

1603 Queen Elizabeth dies, James I becomes King of England and the Chamberlain's Men change their name to The King's Men.

1613 (29 June) The first Globe theatre burns down.

1614 The second Globe theatre is built.

1616 (23 April) Shakespeare dies.

Glossary

Alderman An important man in local government.

Baptized Given a name in a special church service.

Grammar school A school where children were taught Latin, as well as reading and writing.

Leatherworker A person who makes leather goods.

Lent A special time for Christians.

Livery A uniform.

Mayor The most public figure in a town.

Myths Stories about heroes or gods of ancient times.

Plague A terrible disease which killed millions of people.

Playhouse A theatre.

Playwright Someone who writes plays.

Plot The story of a play.

Published Printed as a book.

Further information

Books to read

Life Stories: Shakespeare by Marcella Forster (Wayland, 1995)

The Bard of Avon: The Story of William Shakespeare by Diane Stanley and Peter Vennema (William Morrow and Co., 1992)

Bill S: Shakespeare for Kids by Carole Marsh (Gallopade Publishing Group, 1994)

Shakespeare's Theatre by Jacqueline Morley (Macdonald Young Books, 1994)

BBC Fact Finders: Tudors and Stuarts by Donna Cooper and Bill Cliftlands (BBC Educational Publishing, 1993)

Places to visit

Shakespeare's Globe Exhibition and Shakespeare's Globe Theatre: New Globe Walk, Bankside, London SE1 9ED. Tel: 0171 928 6406.

Shakespeare's birthplace: Henley Street, Stratford-upon-Avon.

Use this book for teaching literacy

This book can help you in the literacy hour in the following ways:

✓ Children can re-tell the story of William Shakespeare to give the main points in sequence and pick out significant incidents.

✓ Teaches children the stories behind part of our heritage, including the words we use. They can also find out about events that were happening in Britain at the time and how they may have influenced the stories.

✓ Children can read simplified stories of Shakespeare's plays and decide what makes them a comedy, tragedy or history.

Index

Numbers in **bold** refer to pictures and text.